# USAIN BOLT

## RECORD-BREAKING SPRINTER

**Simon Hart**

WAYLAND

First published in 2011 by Wayland
Copyright © Wayland 2011

First published in paperback in 2012

Wayland
338 Euston Road
London NW1 3BH

Wayland Australia
Level 17/207 Kent Street
Sydney, NSW 2000

Editor: Nicola Edwards
Designer: Paul Cherrill

British Library cataloguing in
Publication Data
Hart, Simon.
Usain Bolt : record-breaking runner. --
(Inspirational lives)
 1. Bolt, Usain--Juvenile literature.
 2. Runners (Sports)--
 Jamaica--Biography--Juvenile literature.
I. Title II. Series
796.4'22'092-dc22

ISBN: 978 0 7502 6974 2

Printed in China

Wayland is a division of Hachette
Children's Books, an Hachette UK
company.

www.hachette.co.uk

Picture acknowledgements:
The author and publisher would like
to thank the following for allowing
their pictures to be reproduced in this
publication:
Cover: Franck Fife/AFP/Getty Images;
p4 Bill Frakes /Sports Illustrated/
Getty Images; p5 Simon Bruty /Sports
Illustrated/Getty Images; pp6-8 Ian
Walton/Getty Images; p9 Andy Lyons/
Getty Images; p10 Michael Steele/Getty
Images; pp11-12 Jeff Haynes/AFP/Getty
Images; p13 Ian Walton/Getty Images; p14
Michael Steele/Getty Images; p15 Victah
Sailer/Getty Images; p16 Fabrice Coffrini/
AFP/Getty Images; p17 William West/AFP/
Getty Images; p18 Simon Bruty /Sports
Illustrated/Getty Images; p19 AP Photo/
Bryan Cummings, Jamaica Observer; p20
Franck Fife/AFP/Getty Images; p21 Stu
Forster/Getty Images; p22 AP Photo/
Collin Reid; p23 Michael Steele/Getty
Images; p24 Ian Walton/Getty Images;
p25 Alexander Hassenstein/Getty Images
for PUMA; p26 Michael Steele/Getty
Images; p27 SHAUN CURRY/AFP/Getty
Images; p28 AP Photo/Michael Perez; p29
AP Photo/Matt Dunham

# Contents

# The world's fastest human

Usain Bolt is nicknamed 'Lightning Bolt' and in 2008 he showed exactly why. In the space of six astonishing days at the Olympic Games in Beijing, China, the Jamaican sprinter became a sporting superstar. He did so by winning gold medals in the 100 metres and 200 metres before helping his team-mates win the 4x100 metres **relay** title.

## INSPIRATION

"He's an amazing athlete, an inspiration and is great for our sport." Jessica Ennis, British athlete.

*Showing his incredible speed, Usain leaves his rivals trailing to win the 200 metres gold medal in a world record time at the 2009 World Championships in Berlin.*

His day will often begin with a breakfast of saltfish and ackee, a fruit grown in Jamaica. Then, on certain mornings of the week, it is down to the gym for a one-hour workout with lots of exercises involving weights. This is to build up his body strength.

He returns home for lunch. His coach likes him to eat pasta because it is low fat and gives him energy, but sometimes he will have his favourite chicken nuggets.

After resting in front of the TV or playing video games, Usain heads down to the track for afternoon training. The session usually starts at about 4pm when the hot Jamaican sun is not so strong. On a typical day, Usain will do five 200-metre or 150-metre runs. He will finish with a massage to prevent his muscles from stiffening up.

In the evening, Usain often invites friends round to his home for a game of dominoes or to watch football on TV. His favourite team is Manchester United. Usain loves music and dancing and he often used to go out to dance clubs when he was younger. His still goes to clubs occasionally, but not when he is in serious training.

## WOW!

Usain is such a devoted Manchester United fan that, in 2009, he gave Cristiano Ronaldo a sprinting lesson in exchange for a signed shirt. That was before Ronaldo switched to Real Madrid.

Usain shows his love of dance music as he celebrates his three gold medals at the 2009 World Championships at a nightclub in Berlin.

# An inspiration to others

Usain's success on the running track has made him very wealthy and famous but he also wants to be a **role model** for children. When he is not training or competing, he often visits schools at home in Jamaica and elsewhere in the world. His message to the children is to work hard to make their dreams a reality.

## INSPIRATION

"On school visits I tell the children to work hard so they can achieve whatever they want to." Usain Bolt

*A visit to a primary school in Jamaica turns into a game of football between Usain and three young pupils.*

Since becoming a professional athlete in 2003, Usain has also been involved in several charitable projects. In 2009, he set up the Usain Bolt Foundation to raise money for good causes.

In his home community of Trelawny, he has helped improve facilities at his old schools and even lent a hand painting his old infant school, Waldensia Primary. He also bought the school a new television, an air-conditioning system and a computer and he pays the wages of a new teacher in information technology.

Usain has paid for a medical centre in his home village and is planning a play facility. He also aims to provide a proper running water system. At the moment, villagers have to collect their water from rain-water tanks.

Usain has also made donations to charitable projects around the world. After his victories at the Beijing Olympics in 2008, he sent $50,000 to help children injured in the 2008 earthquake disaster in the Chinese province of Sichuan. In 2010, he sent cases of water and clothing to victims of another earthquake on the island of Haiti.

# WOW!

**Usain may be the world's fastest man but he admits he is scared stiff of snakes and biting ants.**

*Usain, now a role model for young people following his record-breaking achievements, goes for a jog with school pupils during a visit to London in 2009.*

# The impact of Usain Bolt

In the years leading up to the Beijing Olympics in 2008, athletics had been going through a very bad time. The reputation of the sport was being ruined by one drug scandal after another when some athletes were found to have been taking banned **performance-enhancing drugs** and many fans were losing interest in the sport. But all that changed when Usain Bolt arrived on the scene.

**TOP TIP**

The best advice I was ever given was to always enjoy the sport. My coach told me that when I was starting out. If you enjoy what you do you can really put your heart into it." Usain Bolt

In the six days it took Usain to win three Olympic gold medals, the sport was transformed. Suddenly, the whole world was interested as Usain's achievements became headline news across the globe. People were no longer talking about drugs and cheating but about how fast Usain could run. Athletics was now seen as something good and positive — all because of one man.

Back in action in 2010, Usain receives the baton from Jamaican team-mate Marvin Anderson as he takes part in a 4x100 metres race at the Penn Relays in Philadelphia.

Usain's success in Beijing, Berlin and Daegu has brought the sport back to life. Fans now turn up in their thousands to catch a glimpse of the giant Jamaican. He has also become a role model for young children who dream about achieving the same success on the running track when they grow up.

But Usain's achievement goes beyond sport. Many people believed there was a limit to how fast a human being could run. Usain has made them think again. He has shown that it is better to think about what is possible, not impossible.

*School pupils strike up Usain's 'lightning bolt' pose with Wenlock, the London 2012 Olympic mascot. The record-beating sprinter is now one of the most famous sports stars on the planet.*

Who knows what the future holds for Usain. He has talked about breaking his world records again. He is also thinking about trying the 400 metres and the long jump. Whatever he does, you can be sure he will do it with a smile on his face. For Usain, sport is always something to be enjoyed.

# INSPIRATION

"Usain is just one hell of a nice guy, a humble man unchanged one little bit by all this glory." Bruce Golding, Prime Minister of Jamaica.

# Have you got what it takes to be a record-breaking athlete?

1) Do you prefer energetic activities to sitting in a chair?
(a) Yes. I'd much rather be running around outside than be cooped up indoors.
(b) It varies. I do like sport and energetic games but I have to be in the mood.
(c) I don't like tiring myself out. I'd rather watch TV.

2) What would you do if you were invited to athletics training after school?
(a) I'd make the most of the opportunity and train and hard as I can to get fitter and faster.
(b) I'd try to go to most training sessions, though maybe not all of them.
(c) Extra PE after school? I'd definitely say no. I couldn't think of anything worse.

3) Usain finds it hard to give up chicken nuggets. Could you give up your favourite food if it helped you run faster?
(a) Yes. You have to make some sacrifices if you want to be the best.
(b) I'd give it a go but I'd probably have to cheat now and then.
(c) No way. There are some foods I just could never give up.

4) Would you be able to cope with pain during a hard training session?
(a) I would like to think so. I know training can be painful sometimes but you have to push yourself.
(b) That depends on how much it hurts. I can cope with some discomfort but I'm not sure about extreme pain.
(c) Absolutely not. Why put yourself through pain if you can avoid it?

5) When you are playing sport, how important to you is winning?
(a) Extremely important. I'm a really bad loser.
(b) I like to win but of course I understand that other people want to win just as much.
(c) I'm not bothered about winning or losing.

6) How nervous are you before a race?
(a) I'm nervous but also excited. I'm anxious to do my best.
(b) Really nervous. I tend to get scared on important occasions.
(c) Not nervous at all. What's the big deal?

7) When you set yourself a goal for the future, how determined are you to achieve it?
(a) Very. I don't like failing at things.
(b) Fairly determined, though you can't achieve every target.
(c) I don't set myself targets. I prefer to live life day by day.

## RESULTS

Mostly As: You have the right kind of attitude to become a record-breaker. Even if you are not the fastest sprinter, there are plenty of other sports that may suit you.

Mostly Bs: You could be successful at sport but the most important thing at this stage is to enjoy it. There is plenty of time to get more serious when you are older.

Mostly Cs: You don't seem cut out to be a record-breaking athlete but you should still try to do some exercise. You may really enjoy it.

30

# Glossary

**ambassador** A high-ranking diplomatic official who represents a country.

**Berlin Wall** The fortified barrier that divided East Germany from West Germany from 1961 to 1989.

**CARIFTA** The Caribbean Free Trade Association.

**coach** A trainer or fitness adviser.

**cramp** A sudden contraction of a muscle, causing severe pain.

**deprived** Lacking the basic necessities of life.

**eliminated** Knocked out of a competition.

**form** Physical condition or fitness.

**gala** Lavish social event or celebration.

**hamstring muscle** One of the three muscles at the back of the upper leg.

**mascot** A person or animal that is meant to bring good luck.

**parish** A district that has its own church.

**performance-enhancing drugs** Substances taken by athletes to make them faster, stronger or to improve their endurance. This is usually against the rules.

**personal best** The best performance an athlete has achieved in his or her entire career.

**prestige** Respect and admiration. Something that is prestigious commands the respect of others.

**professional** Someone who is paid for what they do.

**qualify** To make it through to the next round of a competition.

**relay** A running race for teams of four in which each athlete runs part of the race before passing a baton to the next runner.

**role model** A person who sets an example to others.

**running spikes** Athletes' shoes with metal spikes on the soles to grip the track.

**scholarship** A gift of money to help pay for a student's education.

**scoliosis** A condition in which the spine curves abnormally from side-to-side.

**showmanship** Skill at performing in an entertaining way.

**specialist** Someone who concentrates on one particular activity.

**sponsor** A company that provides financial support to for example, a sportsperson.

**street race** A running race that is held in a street rather than on an athletics track.

# Index

Incredibly, Usain achieved all three victories in world record times, making him the fastest human being in history. He even had time to slow down and celebrate his victory in the 100 metres long before he crossed the finish line. It showed he was capable of running even faster.

A year later, he did exactly that. At the 2009 World Athletics Championships in the German city of Berlin, Usain proved what an amazing athlete he is by beating his own world records in the 100 and 200 metres. He also became the first athlete to hold the Olympic and world records for the 100 and 200 metres at the same time. Aged 23, he was already being described as one of the greatest athletes of all time.

With his 2-metre (6ft 5in) frame, Usain is a sporting giant in every sense. His achievements on the track have made him one of the most famous sports stars in the world. His **showmanship** has added to his popularity. He loves to entertain his fans by playing around before a race and striking his trademark 'lightning bolt' pose afterwards. For Usain, running is all about having fun and enjoying life to the full.

# HONOURS BOARD
## Usain Bolt's medal record

World Junior Championships 2002 (Kingston)
Gold: 200 metres
Silver: 4x100 metres relay
Silver: 4x400 metres relay

World Youth Championships 2003 (Sherbrooke)
Gold: 200 metres

World Championships 2007 (Osaka)
Silver: 200 metres
Silver: 4x100 metres relay

Olympic Games 2008 (Beijing)
Gold: 100 metres (world record)
Gold: 200 metres (world record)
Gold: 4x100 metres relay (world record)

World Championships 2009 (Berlin)
Gold: 100 metres (world record)
Gold: 200 metres (world record)
Gold: 4x100 metres relay (world record)

World Championships 2011 (South Korea)
Gold: 200 metres
Gold: 4x100 metres relay (world record)

*Usain strikes his familiar 'lightning bolt' pose to celebrate his 200 metres gold medal at the 2008 Olympic Games in Beijing.*

# A lively child

Usain St Leo Bolt was born on August 21st, 1986 in Trelawny, a quiet **parish** in the north-west of the Caribbean island of Jamaica. His mother and father, Jennifer and Wellesley Bolt, still live there and run a small grocery shop. Usain has an older half-sister, Christine, and a younger half-brother, Sadiki.

Usain was brought up in simple, two-bedroom rented house. Although his family did not have much money when he was young, he never felt **deprived**. He had a happy, carefree childhood and always had bundles of energy, spending hours playing football and cricket with his friends in the tropical sunshine.

## WOW!

At first, Usain wanted to be a professional cricketer when he grew up. As a boy, he and his friends used to play cricket with an orange for a ball and a banana tree for stumps.

Wellesley Bolt, Usain's father, at work in his small grocery shop in Trelawny, north-west Jamaica.

In fact, Usain was so energetic and unable to stay still for a single moment that Wellesley was worried that there might be something wrong with him and took him to the doctor. The doctor told him not to be concerned. Perhaps all that energy would make him do something great in the future.

Jennifer first noticed Usain's athletic talent when he used to run all the way to school. He was so much faster than the other children. When he was seven, he won his first trophy for running after finishing first in a race at Waldensia Primary School.

Usain was picked for the school athletic team but in those days he preferred playing football and cricket. He was such a good batsman and fast bowler that, at the age of eight, he was playing cricket at school with 11-year-olds. His obvious sporting ability earned him a sports **scholarship** to William Knibb High School – one of the best schools in Trelawny.

# INSPIRATION

"My parents were really supportive. They made sure I got to track meetings and I had everything I needed to train. At the same time, they made sure I trained." Usain Bolt

*Usain's mother, Jennifer, is pictured here outside the Bolt family home in Sherwood Content, Trelawny.*

# Success comes early

Usain's life changed when he was 12 years old. Until then, cricket had been his main interest. Athletics was just a hobby and he often used to skip after-school training sessions to visit a video games shop. But his father, Wellesley, found out about the missed training and was furious. He took Usain to school for a meeting with his teachers. Usain was warned he would lose his sports scholarship unless he tried harder.

**WOW!**

Usain competed at the CARIFTA Games for the second time in 2002 and won two gold medals. The crowd started chanting "Lightning Bolt, Lightning Bolt", which is how Usain got his nickname.

Usain learned his lesson and started training more seriously. Because of his sprinting ability, his school coaches advised him to give up football and cricket to concentrate on athletics. As his performances improved, Usain began to realise he had a real talent for running fast. Success soon followed.

*Pupils of William Knibb High School in Trelawny do their own version of Usain's famous 'lightning bolt' pose. Usain attended the school after being awarded a sports scholarship.*

By the time he was 14, Usain was the best runner in the school. In 2001, he won a silver medal in the 200 metres at the Jamaican High School Championships and silver medals in the 200 and 400 metres at the CARIFTA Games – a competition for Caribbean countries. The same year he was selected for the World Youth Championships in Debrecen, Hungary. Although he failed to **qualify** for the 200 metres final, he set a **personal best** time of 21.73 seconds.

In 2002, aged 15, Usain made a stunning breakthrough at the World Junior Championships, which were being held in Kingston in his own country of Jamaica. The championships were for under-20s but Usain did not look out of place as he was already nearly 2 metres (6ft 5in) tall. In front of an ecstatic home crowd, Usain won the 200 metres gold medal, becoming the youngest athlete ever to win a junior world title. His journey to sprinting greatness had begun.

Usain, aged just 15 years old, enjoys his first major success on the track by winning the world junior 200 metres title in Kingston, Jamaica, in 2002.

## WOW!

Usain was so nervous before the final at the World Junior Championships that he put his running spikes on the wrong feet. Luckily, he realised his mistake before the start of the race.

# Reality check

Usain's victory at the World Junior Championships received lots of coverage in the Jamaican newspapers. The schoolboy sprinter from Trelawny was now famous and the Jamaican public expected great things of him. He did not disappoint his new admirers when he won the 200 metres title at the World Youth Championships in Sherbrooke, Canada, in 2003.

## WOW!

After his success as a junior, Usain was offered scholarships by several American colleges to train in the United States. Usain turned them all down because he wanted to stay at home in Jamaica.

*At the age of 16, Usain clinches another global title as he wins the 200 metres final at the 2003 World Youth Championships in Sherbrooke, Canada.*

Usain left William Knibb High School and moved to Kingston, the Jamaican capital, to train full-time with a **coach** called Fitz Coleman. Things appeared to be going very well for the teenager, despite the disappointment of missing the senior World Championships in Paris in 2003 when an eye infection cut short his training. Having equalled the 200 metres junior world record in 2003, Usain broke it in the early summer of 2004 with a brilliant winning time of 19.93 seconds at the CARIFTA Games in Bermuda.

But as Usain looked forward to competing in his first Olympic Games in Athens in 2004, everything started to go wrong. First he pulled a **hamstring muscle**, then he started to complain of a sore back. An ankle injury added to his problems. When he arrived in Athens, he felt in no fit state to compete. In his first-round heat of the 200 metres, he finished fifth and was **eliminated**. His Olympics were over almost as soon as they had begun.

When Usain returned home to Jamaica, the public were critical of Usain. Some people said he did not have the right attitude and accused him of going out too much at night. For the first time in his life, Usain started to feel very down.

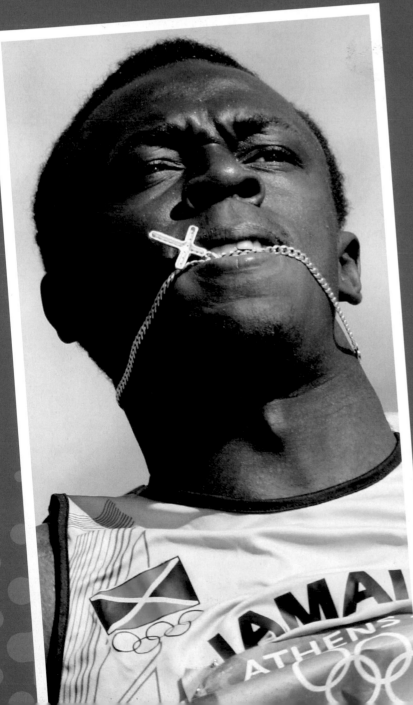

## TOP TIP

"In sport, if you're too aggressive you don't know how it'll end. Although I'm still competitive on the track, I don't believe in aggression. I don't take those kinds of risks. I'm not that kind of guy. I'm a calm, laid-back person." Usain Bolt

*Usain looks tense and disappointed after his performance in the first round of the men's 200 metres during the Olympic Games in Athens in 2004.*

# Time to rebuild

Usain's poor display in Athens proved a turning point. He began to question the tough training methods of his coach, and wondered whether they were the cause of his injury problems. He decided he needed to make a change and began working with the experienced Jamaican team coach, Glen Mills. The pair immediately formed a close bond.

'Mr Mills' – as Usain still calls him – ordered a medical examination to find out why he was getting injured so much. Usain was found to have a condition called **scoliosis**, which causes his spine to curve to the right and makes his right leg a centimetre shorter than his left. The answer was to devise an exercise plan to make his body stronger and more flexible without pushing him too hard.

Usain competed at the World Championships in Helsinki, Finland, in 2005 but his injury problems continued. Although he made it to the 200 metres final, he suffered **cramp** midway through the race and hobbled across the finish line in last place.

*Unhappy times for Usain as he leaves the track on a stretcher after suffering an attack of cramp during the 200 metres final at the 2005 World Championships in Helsinki.*

The rebuilding process carried on in 2006 and Usain decided not to compete at the Commonwealth Games in Melbourne, Australia, after suffering a hamstring strain. Meanwhile, the Jamaican public were growing impatient. People were beginning to question why the sprinter who won the junior world title in 2002 had made so little progress as a senior.

Usain's answer came at the 2007 World Championships in the Japanese city of Osaka. In the final of the 200 metres he won the silver medal behind the American, Tyson Gay, before winning another silver for Jamaica in the relay. After three frustrating years, Usain's injury troubles were behind him at last. Just as importantly, his confidence was returning.

American sprinter Tyson Gay takes the 200 metres gold medal at the 2007 World Championships in Osaka, but Usain is not far behind him in second place.

# The world takes notice

Ever since he started out in athletics, Usain had been a **specialist** 200 metres runner. By 2007, he was keen to try the 100 metres as well. His coach did not believe he was suited to the shorter sprint but agreed to let him run it – on one condition. First he would have to break the Jamaican 200 metres record.

At the Jamaican Championships in June 2007, Usain kept his side of the bargain with a stunning 200 metres run of 19.75 seconds, breaking the 36-year-old national record. After the race, his first words to his coach were: "When is the hundred?"

## WOW!

When Usain ran 9.76 seconds in Kingston, many people believed the clock was faulty. They said it was impossible for him to run so fast.

A month later, Usain was granted his wish when he ran in his first ever senior 100 metres race on the Greek island of Crete. His time of 10.03 seconds was so impressive that Usain's coach agreed to let him run both the 100 and 200 metres the following year.

In the early summer of 2008, in only his third 100 metres race as a senior, Usain ran an incredible time of 9.76 seconds at an athletics meeting in Kingston. It was the second fastest 100 metres time in history. Only fellow Jamaican Asafa Powell had run faster with his world record time of 9.74 seconds.

*Usain is all smiles as he chats to reporters following his brilliant time of 9.76 seconds to win the 100 metres at the Jamaica International in 2008.*

By the end of the month, Usain was the new 100 metres world record-holder. At a meeting in New York, he produced a breathtaking performance to triumph in 9.72 seconds, becoming the fastest sprinter of all time.

Usain was in the best **form** of his life and, in July, ran a personal best of 19.67 seconds to win a 200 metres race in Athens. The Beijing Olympics were fast approaching and Usain was now on a double mission to win 100 and 200 metres gold.

# WOW!

Just before Usain broke the world 100 metres record in New York, the stadium was hit by a huge thunderstorm. It clearly didn't bother the athlete nicknamed "Lightning Bolt".

The electronic clock displays Usain's world-record 100 metres time of 9.72 seconds at the Reebok Grand Prix in New York in 2008. This was the start of Usain's amazing record-breaking spree.

# Olympic superstar

August 16, 2008, will go down as one of the most spectacular moments in the history of athletics. On a sultry night in Beijing, watched by a crowd of 90,000 inside the Bird's Nest stadium, Usain won the Olympic 100 metres final in a new world record time of 9.69 seconds. Even more amazing, he slowed down before the finish.

**WOW!**

During his time in Beijing, Usain lived on chicken nuggets because they were the only food that did not give him a stomach upset. He ate them for breakfast, lunch and dinner.

Leading the race after 60 metres, Usain powered away from his rivals and quickly established a big lead. He was so far ahead of his opponents that he began to celebrate his triumph before the race had even finished, stretching out his arms before pointing to his chest. The stadium erupted as news of his world record flashed up on the scoreboard. Everyone was asking the same question. How much faster could he have gone if he hadn't slowed down before crossing the finish line?

*Usain was looking at the crowd and beginning his celebrations before he even crossed the finish line in the 100 metres final at the 2008 Beijing Olympics. He still set a world record of 9.69 seconds.*

Four days later, Usain returned to the stadium for the final of the 200 metres – the event that had always been his speciality since he was a boy. This time there was no slowing down at the finish. Running as hard as he could, Usain sent the crowd into a frenzy again by winning in a time of 19.30 seconds. He had broken the 12-year-old world record of the great American athlete, Michael Johnson.

Usain was not quite finished. Two days later he won his third Olympic gold medal in the final of the 4x100 metres relay along with his Jamaican team-mates - Michael Frater, Nesta Carter and Asafa Powell. Their winning time was 37.10 seconds: another world record.

*History is made at the 2008 Olympics in Beijing as Usain wins the 200 metres final to clinch his second individual gold medal of the Games. Incredibly, he did so by setting another world record of 19.30 seconds.*

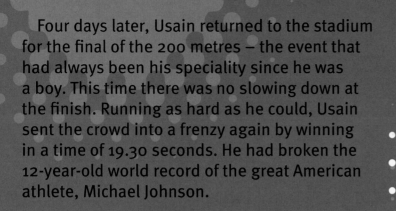

# WOW!

**Bolt's winning margin in the 200 metres final in Beijing was 0.66 seconds. It was the biggest margin of victory since the 200 metres became part of the Olympics in 1900.**

# Return of a hero

After finishing his season in Europe, Usain flew to Jamaica on September 8th for a hero's homecoming. The Jamaican Prime Minister, Bruce Golding, was one of the first people to shake Usain's hand as he stepped out of his aeroplane in Kingston. Thousands of flag-waving fans were also there to greet the new Olympic superstar.

Usain was driven to central Kingston in an open-topped car but so many people were lining the streets that the vehicle made very slow progress. Everyone in the city wanted to congratulate him. Two weeks later, Usain experienced similar scenes when he went home to Trelawny for another public celebration. About 20,000 people turned up for a party at William Knibb High School, where Usain first began training seriously as an athlete.

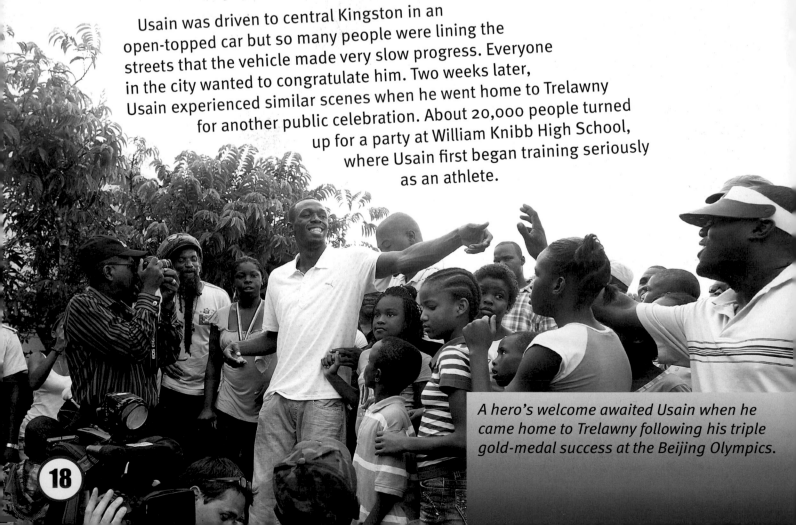

A hero's welcome awaited Usain when he came home to Trelawny following his triple gold-medal success at the Beijing Olympics.

18

The celebrations continued for many more weeks as Usain was invited to countless dinners and award ceremonies. The most prestigious of them took place at glitzy **gala** dinner in Monaco, where Usain was presented with the award of "World Male Athlete of the Year".

The many public appearances meant Usain had to delay the start of his training for the 2009 season. In April 2009, he suffered another interruption to his training. As a reward for his Olympic performances, he had been given a brand-new BMW M3 car by his **sponsor**, Puma.

While driving in wet conditions in Jamaica, Usain lost control of the car, which flipped over three times before landing in a ditch. Luckily, Usain and his two passengers escaped serious injury but Usain cut his feet on sharp thorns while leaving the upturned car. He was unable to run properly for two weeks but it could have been a lot worse.

# WOW!

After the Olympics, Usain thought he had lost his gold medals. He was on a trip on a to New York and left the medals in a bag in a hotel room. Later, he couldn't remember where he left the bag. It took him hours to find it.

Usain is pursued by reporters as he leaves hospital in Jamaica following his car accident in 2009. He was lucky to escape with only minor injuries when his car skidded off a rain-soaked highway.

# Lightning strikes twice

Usain showed he was unaffected by his car crash scare when he was invited to take part in a **street race** on a temporary track in Manchester city centre. Unusually, the race was 150 metres long, which is not an official distance in athletics. It was Usain's first race of 2009 and he won easily in 14.35 seconds. It was the fastest time ever recorded for 150 metres.

The main event of 2009 was the World Championships in Berlin in August. Usain was in great form, recording comfortable victories in 100 and 200 metres races across Europe. Everywhere he competed, huge crowds turned out to watch him in action, especially Jamaican fans living abroad. Reporters and cameramen jostled around him whenever he appeared in public.

## WOW!

Usain broke the 200 metres world record in Berlin on his 23rd birthday. It was another birthday present to add to the 200m Olympic title that he won on the eve of his 22nd birthday.

*A year after his triple success at the Beijing Olympics, Usain won three more gold medals at the 2009 World Championships in Berlin, finishing with the 4x100 metres relay.*

In Berlin, Usain faced tough competition from America's Tyson Gay, who had been injured in Beijing. But Usain was not about to be upstaged. Astonishingly, he won the final of the 100 metres in 9.58 seconds, smashing the world record that he had set at the Olympics by more than a 10th of a second. The 100 metres world record had never been lowered by so much in a single race.

Before the final of the 200 metres, Usain said he was feeling too tired to the break the world record again, but there was no stopping the world's fastest man. Once again, he beat his own world record, winning in an incredible time of 19.19 seconds. He celebrated by dancing around with the **mascot** of the championships, Berlino the Bear.

Usain finished the championships with a third gold medal in the 4x100 metres relay, just as he done at the Olympics the year before. He was now a triple Olympic and triple world champion and had rewritten the record books yet again.

## HONOURS BOARD
### 100 metres world records

- *9.58 seconds: Usain Bolt (Jamaica) August 16 2009*
- *9.69 seconds: Usain Bolt (Jamaica) August 16 2008*
- *9.72 seconds: Usain Bolt (Jamaica) May 31 2008*
- *9.74 seconds: Asafa Powell (Jamaica) September 9 2007*
- *9.77 seconds: Asafa Powell (Jamaica) June 11 2006*
- *9.77 seconds: Justin Gatlin (United States) May 12 2006*
- *9.77 seconds: Asafa Powell (Jamaica) June 14 2005*
- *9.79 seconds: Maurice Greene (United States) June 16 1999*
- *9.84 seconds: Donovan Bailey (Canada) July 27 1996*
- *9.85 seconds: Leroy Burrell (United States) July 6 1994*
- *9.86 seconds: Carl Lewis (United States) August 25 1991*
- *9.90 seconds: Leroy Burrell (United States) June 14 1991*

*Usain, second from right, celebrates with his three Jamaican team-mates following their relay triumph at the 2009 World Championships in Berlin.*

# Awards and injuries

After Usain's success at the World Championships, the awards came thick and fast. The city of Berlin presented him with a section of the **Berlin Wall** with his picture painted on it to ship home to Jamaica. It was two metres high and weighed two tonnes! He was also crowned 'World Male Athlete of the Year' for the second year running.

Back home, the Jamaican Government presented Usain with the prestigious Order of Jamaica, which is the country's fourth highest honour. It means he is now an **ambassador** of Jamaica and his official title is 'Honourable Usain St Leo Bolt'.

**WOW!**

In honour of Usain's achievements, Jamaican Prime Minister Bruce Golding renamed a road on the island the 'Usain Bolt Highway'. It is the same road where Usain crashed his car in 2009.

*In recognition of his athletics achievements, Usain receives the Order of Jamaica from the country's Governor General, Sir Patrick Allen.*

Because there was no major championship in 2010, Usain announced that he would be taking things a little easier to allow his body to recover from the previous two seasons.

After winning his first few races in 2010 he suffered an ankle injury and had to rest. He returned to action a month later but his doctor advised him to run only 100 metres races to avoid making the injury worse.

Usain won races in Switzerland and Paris but then suffered his first defeat in two years. He was beaten by his American rival, Tyson Gay, in a 100 metres race in Sweden. Afterwards, Usain revealed that he had injured his back. On medical advice, he decided to end his season early to avoid causing any further damage.

In 2011, at the World Championships in Daegu, South Korea, Usain came back fit and strong, winning Gold in the 200 metres and breaking yet another world record to win gold in the 4x100 metres relay.

## HONOURS BOARD
### Usain's awards

*Order of Jamaica: 2009*

*IAAF World Athlete of the Year: 2008 & 2009*

*Laureus World Sportsman of the Year: 2009 & 2010*

*BBC Overseas Sports Personality of the Year: 2008 & 2009*

*Track and Field News Athlete of the Year: 2008 & 2009*

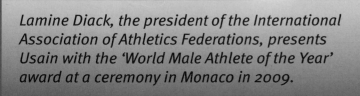

*Lamine Diack, the president of the International Association of Athletics Federations, presents Usain with the 'World Male Athlete of the Year' award at a ceremony in Monaco in 2009.*

23

# A day in the life of Usain Bolt

The six months from November to April are very important for Usain. That is his training period when he has to work hard on his fitness at home in Kingston to prepare for the athletics season. He needs to be in peak condition by the time summer arrives.

## WOW!

In 2009 Usain adopted a three-month-old cheetah cub in Kenya and named him 'Lightning Bolt'. The cheetah is the world's fastest animal, with a top speed of 105 km/h. Usain's top speed is about 40 km/h.

*To make sure he is in peak physical condition, Usain is given a massage following a training session on his home track in Kingston, Jamaica.*